Stella's Dream

Written by
Lindsey Pope

Illustrated by
Nadja Bullis

Dedicated to my Mom, Jane. Thank you for shining so brightly in my life and the lives of many others.

"Hello there, my dear friends!"
Stella swims in the sea.
"A pirate's treasure chest!
So much fun for me!"

She finds three coins inside the chest,
They each depict a fish.
Each reads: Bring me from shore to sea
I'll grant you one true wish.

Inside she holds a secret close
that she's never dared to tell.
She watches stars up in the sky
and dreams to glow as well.

She makes a promise to herself,
"Today will be for me!
At last I'll be a glowing star,
I'll bring my wish to sea!"

Sheldon plops right next to her
and suddenly declares,

"Please grant my wish, it's meaningful
There's nothing that compares!"

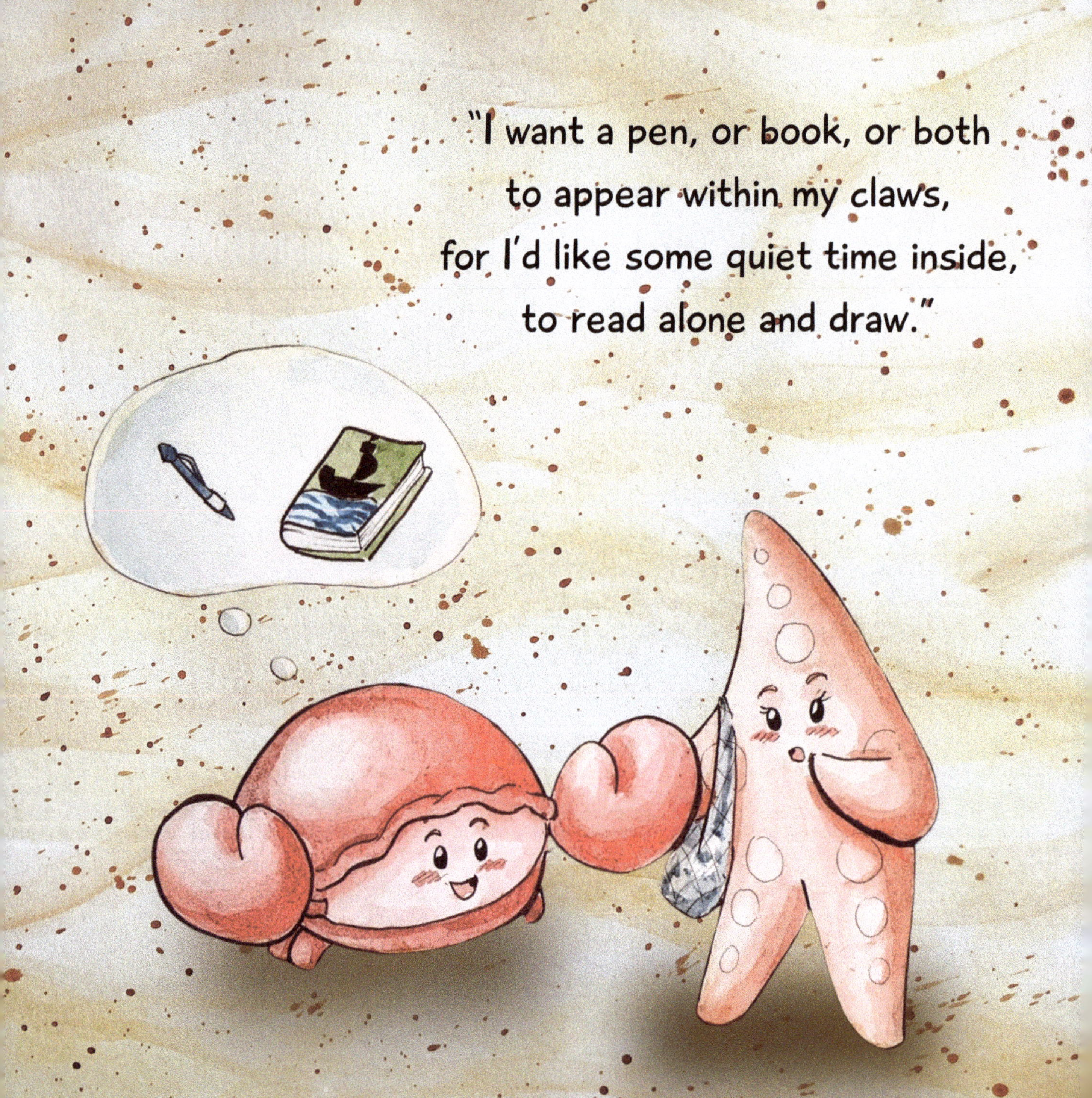
"I want a pen, or book, or both
to appear within my claws,
for I'd like some quiet time inside,
to read alone and draw."

So Stella grabs one coin and swims
out to the ocean blue.
She's on a mission for her friend
to help his wish come true.

When she returns back home at last she sees
the next coin as her chance.

She recites her promise to herself
and does a happy dance.

She repeats her promise with a smile,
"Today will be for me!
At last I'll be a glowing star,
I'll take my wish to sea."

Then Sully lands right next to her
and suddenly declares.
"Let's grant my wish, it's meaningful!
There's nothing that compares!"

"I've felt like a small bird since birth.
I feel though, that is wrong.

I want to wake feeling more like
an eagle, bold and strong."

She swims fast and returns so tired,
"I hope it's now my chance."
It's time to say her promise, but,
she's too sleepy now to dance.

She recalls her dream with all her might.
"At last, this coin's for me,
for once I'll be a glowing star
I'll take my wish to sea!"

She drags herself toward the shore
"A sleepy star, that's me."

Her eyes close shut, she falls asleep
before she's reached the sea.

Her friends awake her after dawn
"Oh, what a lovely day!"
They're full of joy to see their friend,
they cannot wait to play.

But Stella cannot find her coin
she searches far and wide.
"My coin! My dream! It cannot be,
"It's washed out with the tide!"

"I'm glad I helped your wishes go out
and took your dreams to sea.
I guess it's time I should accept...
no dream is left for me."

Sully calls to mind some sea glass
   he'd found on rocks below

might just create a necklace
and help her seem to glow.

In scrambling to surprise their friend,
she asks them, "What's the rush?"

While handing her the necklace
they say, "You always glow to us."

Stella smiles while slowly glancing down
"I sparkle like the sea!

There's no need to dream of evening stars
for I glow...just being me."

The End

Did you enjoy Stella's Dream? Be sure to check out Sheldon's Time!

www.ingramcontent.com/pod-product-compliance
Lightning Source LLC
Chambersburg PA
CBHW040226110726

48005CB00024B/2820